NORTHEAST PASSAGE

NORTHEAST PASSAGE

A Photographer's Journey Along the
Historic Northern Forest Canoe Trail

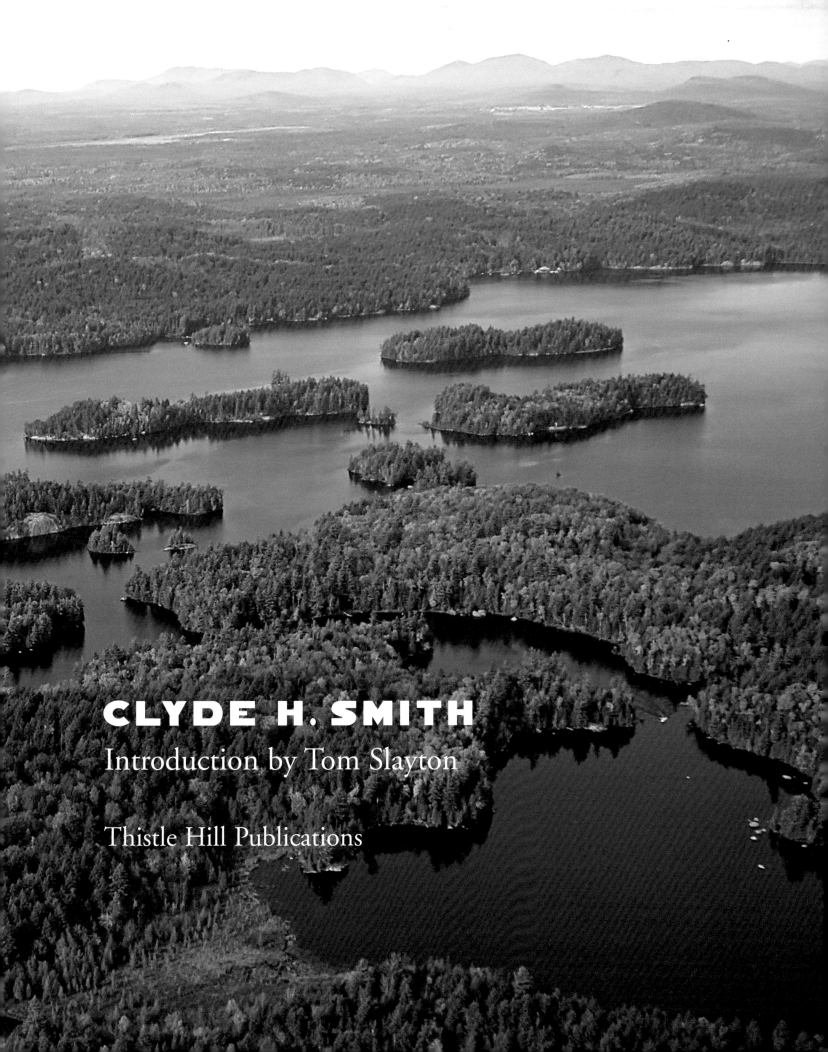

CLYDE H. SMITH

Introduction by Tom Slayton

Thistle Hill Publications

Publication of this book was made possible by financial assistance from the Avenir Foundation, established by descendants of Homer Dodge, including his daughter, Alice Dodge Wallace. We are grateful for their support.

Northeast Passage by Clyde H. Smith

Copyright © 2007, Clyde H. Smith

Photography and illustrations by Clyde H. Smith

Photographs edited by Clyde H. Smith

Design by The Laughing Bear Associates, Montpelier, Vermont

Photography reproduction enhancement by David Goodman

Printing by Spectrum Graphics, Portland, Maine

THISTLE HILL PUBLICATIONS
Post Office Box 307, North Pomfret, Vermont 05053
Jack Crowl, publisher

ISBN: 978-0-9705511-4-6

Page 1: Migrating snow geese
Pages 2-3: Upper, Middle and Lower Saranac Lakes, New York
Pages 7-8: The Abbey Rapids of the Missisquoi River at Sheldon, Vermont, looking east toward Jay Peak

CONTENTS

Homer Dodge, Colorado River, Utah

Known as the "dean of American canoeing," Homer Dodge explored
many great rivers during his colorful career. Clyde Smith spent
a month on the Colorado River with Dodge in 1972, retracing the steps
of explorer John Wesley Powell's 1869 route through the canyons
of Utah and Arizona.

HOMER DODGE:
'BORN IN A CANOE'

My first glimpse of Homer Dodge was in the early 1960s. I was walking the streets of Burlington, Vermont with a friend, discussing the burgeoning new sport of white-water canoeing. The name of Homer Dodge often came up while talking about running the rivers in those days. So it was providential that he just happened to be driving by in his Jeep station wagon while we were in that conversation. However, I was somewhat disconcerted to see a mashed carcass of a metal canoe on his Jeep's roof. It was clearly the remains of a Grumman aluminum canoe, its painted lettering still showing at one end.

I was in Burlington to attend a meeting of the newly formed "Canoe Cruisers of Northern Vermont." It was an opportunity to become a charter member, and I had learned that Homer Dodge was its inspirational advisor. But I was apprehensive after seeing the remains of Homer's boat on the roof of his Jeep.

How, I wondered, did he ever survive such destruction with his canoe and still be able to walk around?

The story slowly came to light at that first meeting. It turned out that Homer had just returned from a Western trip where he paddled some of the great canyon rivers in Utah. Having completed

Androscoggin River, New Hampshire

Homer Dodge demonstrates his double-blade skill in a downriver race on a section of what would later become the Northern Forest Canoe Trail.

a successful journey by canoe, he decided to take a shortcut on the way home to explore some old mining roads in Utah's Henry Mountains. While negotiating one narrow section, soft sand on the road's shoulder suddenly gave away and Homer's Jeep rolled over several times, with his canoe still strapped to its top! It finally came to rest on its side at the very edge of an abyss, within a whisker of a 500-foot freefall to the canyon floor below. After extracting himself from the vehicle, Homer walked for miles to find

a group of miners who returned with him the following morning and winched his Jeep up from the precipice. Homer then drove to Colorado, got a few broken ribs patched up, then finished the drive back to Vermont.

As advisor to the "Canoe Cruisers," Homer Dodge accompanied the group on many rivers throughout the northeast. We explored almost every navigable river in the region. Homer taught us to study the rapids before making any difficult runs. Often sitting on a bank, sometimes munching our lunch, we would listen to the roar of the rapids and study the souse holes and swirling eddies around boulders. Homer might say, "We'll run this one by following the smart log!" With that, he would toss a lengthy stick into the river and we would watch it float with the current, missing all the obstacles. Back in our canoes, we followed the line of the "smart log." Most of the time it was clear sailing, but I remember one occasion when, on reaching the bottom of the rapids, I found the log hung up on a boulder. "Sometimes you've gotta make snap decisions," Homer shouted as he careened around the rock, flailing his double-bladed paddle and expertly avoiding a collision in his newly acquired Grumman canoe.

Unbeknownst to me was the slick marketing method Homer had devised to get the Grumman Company to provide him with a shiny new canoe. The heap of crushed metal atop his Jeep with "Grumman Aluminum Canoe" printed upside down for the entire world to see was bad PR for the company. So Homer took the opportunity to request a new canoe, this time a shorter, 15-footer that was easier to maneuver when he was running rapids as a single paddler.

One of Homer's dictums was, "The trick for running big water is to paddle backwards. That way the canoe's bow doesn't dive into the troughs and fill up after cresting a wave." Paddling back-

wards is a technique that often makes the difference between emerging from a rapid right side up or upside down.

It seemed to us that Homer Dodge must have been born in a canoe. His trademark was that double-bladed paddle. And he often wore a necktie under his life jacket. His river running career had begun years earlier on the St. Lawrence in Canada, where he ran rapids in a small skiff. Many years later, during the construction of the St. Lawrence Seaway, Homer ran an open canoe down the thrashing Long Sault Rapids one last time before they were silenced forever by the seaway diversion.

When the Seaway was opened, he escorted the heavy cruiser, the USS Macon — all 674 feet of it — through the Eisenhower Lock, in his 15-foot canoe. It was an awesome sight.

It is with pride that I dedicate this book to my canoeing mentor, Dr. Homer L. Dodge, former president of Norwich University in Vermont, who was known as the dean of American canoeing. Dr. Dodge's knowledge of rivers and waterway navigation transcends all others of his time. It was a rare privilege for me to share many adventures, in the east as well as on western rivers, with my dear friend, Homer Dodge.

Clyde Smith

Colorado River, Utah

Homer Dodge's favorite breakfast, strawberries and shredded wheat, fortifies him before he sets out for another day on the river with Clyde Smith.

Flagstaff Lake and the Bigelow Range, from Eustis, Maine

This lake was created in 1949 by the flooding of the Dead River when Long Falls Dam was built, submerging three small villages.

THE WAYS OF NATURE

Clyde Smith's face lights up and his gestures become animated when he discusses the Northern Forest Canoe Trail. He wants you to understand just how wonderful the trail really is. "A canoe, to me, is a way of penetrating nature's world. You'd just be amazed at the places you can go quietly in a canoe," he declares.

From the dark, rippling streams of the Adirondacks to the broad sunlit reaches of Moosehead Lake in northern Maine, Smith has paddled much of the Northern Forest Canoe Trail himself. Though he's now in his mid-70s, age hasn't dimmed his enthusiasm for wilderness paddling a bit. And he believes that the recently established canoe trail is one of the best ways to get to know the wild lands of the North Country.

Smith has watched as a family of otters played beside his canoe in a Vermont stream, and has paddled alongside a deer swimming across remote Chamberlain Lake in Maine. He has guided his boat down the briskly flowing waters of the bog-fed Nulhegan River in Vermont's Northeast Kingdom, and has ridden the big standing waves and ferocious whitewater of the Dead River in Maine. Throughout his life he has been attracted to the wild waters of northern New England, and he knows them well.

A constant companion to Smith — in addition to his steadfast canoeing partner and wife, Elizabeth — has been his camera. Clyde Smith is one of the outstanding wildlife and nature photographers of his generation. He has published nearly two dozen books of photographs depicting beautiful, unspoiled places, from his beloved New England to the wilds of Alaska. Recently, he has spent much of each year capturing the beauty of the Northern Forest Canoe Trail. Many of his best images are included in this book.

Smith's understanding of the ways of nature comes easily to him because of his upbringing. He literally grew up on the slopes of New Hampshire's Cardigan Mountain, where his father was a fire warden in the 1930s. He has hiked most of the mountains of New England, discovered an unusual rock formation on Vermont's Mount Mansfield, and named it Cantilever Rock. His entire life has been spent close to nature, and his photographs clearly express his love and understanding of the natural world.

Born in Gorham, N.H. in August, 1931, Smith became a mountain dweller at the tender age of two. His father became the Mount Cardigan fire ranger in 1933, and moved his family to a log cabin high on the mountain. The family went to Florida for the winter months, but for the rest of the year, April to November, they lived on the mountain. They were there, in fact, when the great Hurricane of September 1938 tore a vast swath of destruction through the forests of New England.

"Our cabin was anchored to the stone bedrock of the mountain by big, heavy chains," Smith recalled. "The wind would pick the cabin up but the chains held and that's how we rode out the

storm all night—the noise was terrifying. But we didn't blow away."

The hurricane uprooted and toppled trees all over the mountain. It took Smith's family weeks to reestablish the trail off the mountain.

However, most of his life on Cardigan was less dramatic, but always challenging and fascinating. Smith remembers walking three and one-half miles to school—on snowshoes—in the deep, late-winter snows on the mountain in April. He would arrive back at the cabin at the end of a long walk each day, soaking wet from the melting snow.

Smith first got hooked on canoeing as a camper and later as a teenage counselor at Camp Mowglis on Newfound Lake in rural New Hampshire. Located right at the southern entrance to the White Mountains and directly adjacent to the beautiful New Hampshire lakes country, it was the perfect spot for a budding outdoorsman to get his fill of nature.

Smith had to put away his canoeing for a time when he majored in forestry at the University of New Hampshire. In 1951, at the height of the Korean War, he joined the Air Force, and served for four years. He later worked as an architect in Topeka, Kansas, but moved back to New England—Burlington, Vermont—in 1959.

It was shortly after that, in the early 1960s, that Smith met the man who

Balsam Fir Sprig

would become his canoeing mentor, Homer Dodge, president emeritus of Norwich University and an avid white-water canoeist.

At about the same time, Smith got interested in photography in a serious way. He published his first photograph in *Vermont Life* in 1967. It was a shot of himself, rappelling off the face of Camel's Hump. He was engaged in a variety of outdoor sports at the time, and the then-editor of *Vermont Life*, Walter Hard, suggested that Smith get a large-format camera and take more outdoor photos for the magazine.

Smith liked the idea, but didn't like the thought of carrying a large camera on

his back through the wilderness. So he bought a top-quality 35mm camera. That decision, plus his passion for the outdoors, and what proved to be an unerring eye for photographic color and composition, helped him become a stunningly effective outdoor photographer, one of the first of the new wave of photographers who made top-quality images with 35mm cameras. He sold many photos to *Vermont Life*, and other publications over the next 30 years, published more than 20 books of photos and became a regular contributor to several magazines, including *Skiing* magazine, where he was a photo contributor for 15 years.

Allagash Wilderness Waterway, near Umsaskis Lake, Maine

Paddlers on a misty morning cross a remote section of the Northern Forest Canoe Trail. The Allagash Wilderness Waterway was officially named as the first state-adminstered Wild and Scenic River in 1966.

Smith still travels regularly on photo assignments, but much of his work, since he entered his 70s, has been documenting wilderness and wildlife along the Northern Forest Canoe Trail. The trail has become a passion of his later years and Smith loves paddling on it, promoting it, and talking about it.

"We've got some tremendous places in New England, and they're most easily explored by canoe," he says. "I want people to be aware of the things that are out there in the wild places. Little things like delicate rare plants and flowers such as sundew and pitcher plants."

Or big things like moose and loons and beavers. While he has made many beautiful photographs of New England wildlife, he has a special affinity for the beaver. He's made many photographs of them at work and play, and sometimes decorates the top margins of his care-fully typewritten letters with precise sketches of tiny beavers, doing their woodsy thing.

"They're my symbol of the northern waters," Smith says. "Because they made this country!"

How so? Beavers throughout the various watersheds traversed by the Northern Forest Canoe Trail cut down trees and dam up the little mountain streams (and sometimes the bigger valley streams as well), creating impoundments that retain the region's fast-flowing water through dry times and wet times, releasing it gradually, thus keeping the streams flowing and viable as canoe waterways for most of the year. Only when winter locks the streams in ice does canoeing have to stop. Historically, beavers were an important part of the region's 19th century economy, Smith notes. They were trapped and their fur sold for beaver top hats, coats and other uses, drawing explorers, trappers, and traders to the region. Once trapped relentlessly, beavers have made a major comeback and are once again part of the forest ecology of the North Country.

It's the wide variety of terrain and ecosystems along the Northern Forest Canoe Trail that keeps Smith coming back to photograph it and canoe on it. On its route between Old Forge, N.Y., and Fort Kent at the northernmost tip of Maine, the 740-mile long trail traverses some of the wildest and most remote parts of northern New England and upstate New York. But it's never too far from many of the towns and villages along the way — places like Saranac Lake, N.Y., Island Pond, Vt., Rangeley and Greenville, Maine. Likewise, some sections of the trail send paddlers down serious whitewater rivers, while other sections meander through gentle, winding streams or cross broad lakes. In Island Pond, paddlers can cross the pond, which is wide and serene, or paddle right into the heart of the village — the trail passes directly under the Clyde River Hotel!

"Sometimes you're paddling through great big landscapes, where you feel connected to something very expansive. Other times, you're on intimate little streams and you feel as though you're discovering it for the first time," said Kate Williams, executive director of the NFCT.

"It's a completely varied experience," says Clyde Smith. "That's what makes it so great."

He is enthusiastic about the trail not only for its variety and beauty, but because he believes it will help connect people to the natural world — something we all need. Smith also is confident that the number of people using the trail will continue to grow in years ahead — a good thing both for the people who experience nature while out on the trail, and for the ecological health of the Northern Forest. One goal of both Smith and Williams is to encourage eco-tourism along the trail, thereby benefiting the economy of the communities through which the trail passes.

Smith, who watched the popularity of hiking grow along with the creation of the Appalachian Trail, thinks that the Northern Forest Canoe Trail is poised to help promote canoeing in the same way.

"It's going to grow by leaps and bounds," he predicts. "People of all abilities can use it, and connect to nature through it."

And that, for Clyde Smith, is what it's really all about.

Tom Slayton
Editor Emeritus
Vermont Life

Osprey — also known as a fish hawk

Lake Umbagog National Wildlife Refuge, New Hampshire

Paddlers are often able to enjoy a tranquil moment in this
refuge that straddles the New Hampshire-Maine border.
A variety of waterfowl and wildlife—loon, bald eagle,
osprey, moose, and more—call the refuge home.

A LIQUID CONNECTOR

The Northern Forest Canoe Trail is perhaps best described as a liquid connector. Flowing 740 miles from the western edge of the Adirondack Park to the northern tip of Maine, it connects watersheds, communities, states, countries, ideas, and landscapes. It is a clear thread weaving through the Northern Forest ecosystem — at 30 million acres it is the largest ecosystem east of the Mississippi River.

Most importantly, the trail is a connector of people — to each other, to innumerable special places along its route, and to a rich heritage of stories that shape the Northern Forest region.

We have been honored by Clyde Smith's interest in and affection for the Northern Forest Canoe Trail, and for his unflagging faith in the project of making this Trail a reality. His images are part of our 13-map series and our first book, *Paddling Through Time*, and in their warmth and intimacy, have helped transform what was a big idea into an accessible recreation and heritage resource.

In this book, Clyde's photos transform this resource into a treasure. When he first approached me with his book idea in late summer 2006, I was intrigued — who better to do such a book for us? But

**Connecticut River,
New Hampshire**

Canoeists explore a serene
Connecticut River lagoon
at daybreak.

Opposite:
A hovering osprey spreads
and cups its tail feathers.

I also felt some trepidation. Would we be able to pull it off, in the midst of everything else our small staff does to sustain this extensive trail? Clyde was persistent, and through a series of meetings he dispelled every one of my hesitations and found the generous funding that ultimately made it all possible.

In bringing this project to life, Clyde distinguished himself as a connector on par with the Trail itself. He reminded me — and in this book he reminds us all — of the value of using your gifts on behalf of what you are passionate about as a way to make a difference in the world.

He put it this way in a letter to me: "Through the book, it is my desire to make people aware of what's out there available to us now — to see, hear, smell, and be aware of our place in the cosmos. The Northern Forest Canoe Trail is a gift, the common thread for all those who wish to expand their knowledge about creation."

I believe that Clyde has succeeded in his desire for the book. To him, we offer our deepest gratitude.

Kate Williams
Executive Director
Northern Forest Canoe Trail

NORTHEAST PASSAGE

NORTHERN FOREST CANOE TRAIL

A 740-mile northern waterway
traversing New York, Vermont, Québec,
New Hampshire, and Maine

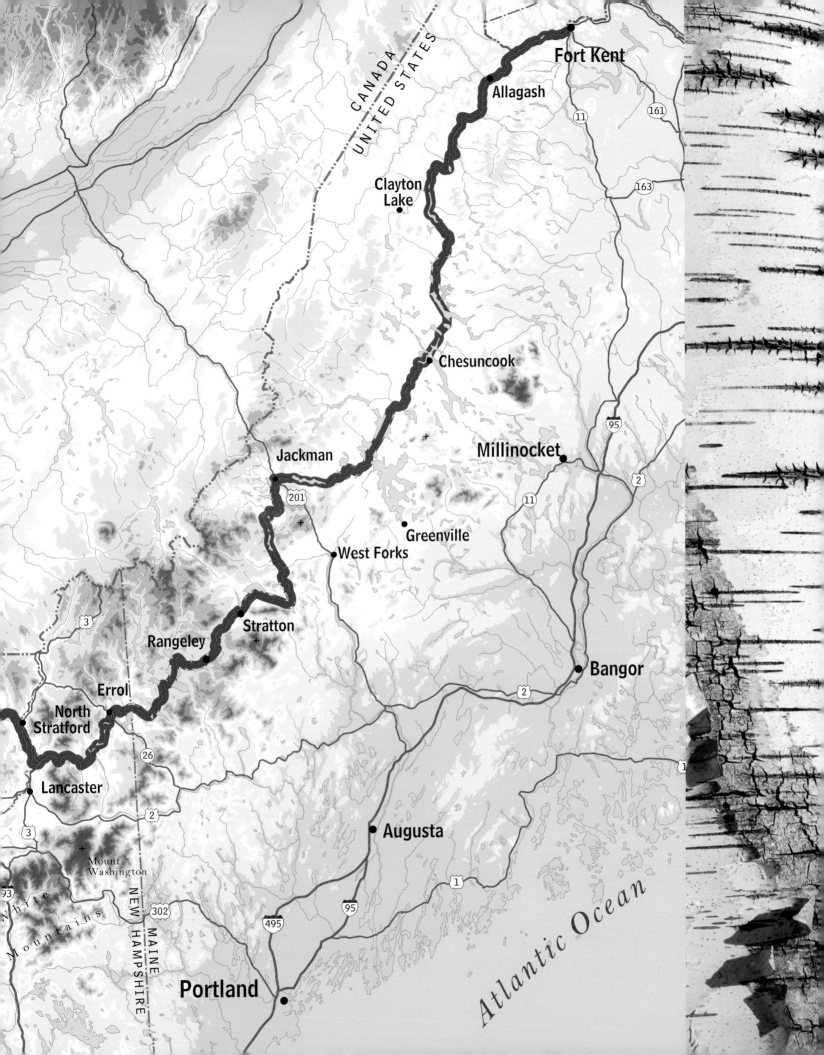

Fort Kent

Allagash

11

161

Clayton
Lake

163

Chesuncook

95

Millinocket

2

Jackman

201

11

Greenville

West Forks

Stratton

Rangeley

Bangor

Errol

North
Stratford

2

Lancaster

26

1

2

Augusta

3

302

1

Mount
Washington

495

95

93

White

Mountains

NEW HAMPSHIRE

MAINE

Portland

Atlantic Ocean

CANADA
UNITED STATES

ICE OUT!

AuSable River, New York

The power of an ice breakup is awesome, as seen here in this stream near the Northern Forest Canoe Trail.

Previous pages: Nulhegan River, Vermont

ICE OUT!

It begins with a single drop of melt water. It may be somewhere in the Adirondack High Peaks, Vermont's Green Mountains, the Whites of New Hampshire, or — a few weeks later — up the northern Appalachian chain to the tip of Maine. Beginning with that single drop, the inevitable process we call Ice Out begins. At first, it is barely a whisper, a shrinking of the snow pack, dripping and groaning below millions of tons of white stuff that will soon turn to white water. It has been that way for eons. Ancient travelers depended upon it as surely as coastal inhabitants' routines are regulated by ocean tides.

But soon the melting becomes intense and anything but quiet. Anyone who has witnessed the power of an ice breakup in a Northeast river can never forget it. Huge ice chunks relentlessly chewing away at shorelines and trees as the water rises are an incredible sight; the noise can be frightening. And they often leave massive destruction in their wake as they roar through river communities. Only after the ice has ground itself to bits and water levels have receded do the rivers regain their normally friendly composure.

Long before the coming of the horse or the invention of the automobile, water routes provided a means for commerce and exploration. Native Americans used the waterways for trade routes the way we

The Black Branch of the Nulhegan River, Vermont
A father and son thread the needle on a difficult drop.

A camp on the Black Branch of the Nulhegan River, Vermont

use present day interstate highways. A number of old books and documents tell of those early exploits along the northern forest canoe routes.

My experience with the sport began in the 1960s, when I had an opportunity to explore many New England and Adirondack waterways. Spring canoeing and kayaking grew in popularity in tandem with the explosion of the winter ski industry in the Northeast. When the snow and ice began to melt, skiers and hangers-on headed for the newly opened waterways.

In those days, canoeing and kayaking centered around competition, with frequent "white-water derbies." Folks would come from far and wide to participate, or simply to be riverbank spectators at the events. Some of the early races took place on the Upper Hudson in North Creek, New York. At about the same time, Vermont held its competition on the West River below the Ball Mountain Dam at Jamaica. Releases from the dam provided a reliable water level for paddlers and spectators as well. Not to be outdone, New Hampshire held white-water races on the Androscoggin in Errol. But the king of all downriver races took place on Maine's Dead River in the shadow of the Bigelow Range. There, dependable water levels could be regulated by releases from the dam at Flagstaff Lake. The longest uninterrupted stretch of white water rapids in the Northeast provided plenty of action in a wilderness setting.

Dead River, Maine

Those competitive events were the evolutionary stepping stones that ultimately led to widespread recreational canoe and kayak paddling. It's a bit like the transition in downhill skiing to cross-country and back-country exploration. And, similar to the skiing industry's dependence on snow-making, some river systems still rely on periodic dam releases in order to have navigable waterways later in the season.

The voyagers of old did not have dam releases to help them, so often it was brute strength that powered their crafts over sandbars and rugged portages. For them, the waterway routes were a matter of necessity. Knowing the route was a vital part of navigation. There were no maps available, so we can only marvel at the ancients' ability to know exactly where they were. Without today's GPS waypoints, folks simply had to rely on their experience and their wits. (We could use a few more of those skills these days!)

The emergence of the Northern Forest Canoe Trail provides a wonderful opportunity to taste some of nature's offerings. And the canoe or kayak provides a convenient vehicle for the observant paddler. The key to tranquility begins with a craft that's propelled without a motor. Creatures of the wild are not usually disturbed by a craft gliding smoothly over a quiet surface. That's when magical encounters with wildlife begin. Within these pages, it is my privilege to share some of the magic that my camera and I have witnessed over the years. Many of the images captured have stories of their own. Here are a few of them.

Raquette River, New York

While furious spring rapids rage in the bigger rivers, smaller tributaries often remain frozen, with meltwater flowing over their surfaces.

Opposite:
Rousing rapids propel another father and son team on a wild ride. This section of the Dead River contains the longest uninterrupted stretch of rapids in the Northeast.

Buds and the first blossoms of wild apple trees

The St. John River, at Fort Kent, Maine

White birches were the raw material used by Native Americans to make their canoes. Native peoples also used the bark for many other things, such as containers and vessels to carry food, water, and items of clothing.

Cow moose

Umbagog Lake, straddling the New Hampshire-Maine border

Creatures of the wild are not usually disturbed by a craft gliding over a quiet surface. That's when magical encounters with wildlife begin.

Swan in Swanton, Vermont

Canada Geese

A family of Canada Geese and goslings, accompanied
by a surrogate parent, cruise a peaceful waterway
in a protective formation. The short Northern Forest
spring and summer gives most creatures only one shot
at raising their young.

Whitetailed deer

Deer are frequent browsers along the shorelines of the Northern Forest Canoe Trail waterways. It is not unusual — but always a thrill — to see them swimming across rivers and even longer distances across lakes.

A wild turkey gobbler

Missisquoi River, Vermont
The 6,642-acre Missisquoi
National Wildlife Refuge, where
the Missisquoi River enters
Lake Champlain, is a mecca
for migrating waterfowl, and is
home to the largest great blue
heron rookery in Vermont.

Purple Trillium — also called Wake-Robin or "Stinkin' Benjamin"

The pussy willow, a harbinger of spring

Bloodroot, named for its root system, which contains bright red juice

Morning dew on a spider's web

The canoe or kayak provides
a convenient vehicle for the
observant paddler.

Willoughby River, Vermont

Rainbow trout fight their way upstream to spawn
in this tributary of the Northern Forest Canoe Trail.

Opposite: Many fishermen practice "catch
and release," but others enjoy a fresh catch
as a highlight of a spring camping experience.

Dead River, Maine

Allagash River, Maine

SUMMER MAGIC

SUMMER MAGIC

In midsummer, my favorite time of day is dawn. The sun has not yet shown itself, but there is a blush on the horizon. Dark spikes of black spruce line the waterway where I launch my canoe, which glides smoothly into the stream as if on spun silk.

I can sense the tug of the river current drawing my craft away from shore as I watch the swirling vapor form twisting columns of mist wafting upward from the water's surface. The whisper of drips sliding off my paddle is the only sound I can hear.

Ahead is a forested peninsula. From the opposite side, still out of sight, a loud splash breaks the silence. It sounds like something big! Was it a moose or just the slap of a beaver's tail — or perhaps even an osprey diving for its breakfast of fish? Alas, as I paddle around the point, all I can see through the morning fog is rippling water.

I'll never discover exactly what caused the splash. But my consolation is that there will be other mornings when nature's grand show will reveal itself.

There are many more magical, even mystical moments a canoeist encounters regularly in summertime paddling. Here are a few of them:

• *The call of a loon, or several loons, "talking" to one another.* The best word I can find for describing their sound is haunting. The loon also produces a number of different yodels. I've heard at least 10 different such sounds at different times of the year.

Upper Ammonooscuc River, New Hampshire

A tundra-like landscape on this section of the trail
is explored by two paddlers.

Top: Fireweed; Bottom: Blue Flag Iris

Great Blue Heron

• *The spectacle of an osprey fishing from the sky.* This giant fish hawk hovers in place while zeroing in on its prey, then plummets into the water like a meteor, only to emerge from under water just as suddenly, with a fish in its talons or beak. Then, flying away with its prize, it shakes like a dog, releasing a great shower of water.

• *The evening dance of the fireflies.* To wander through a field on a dark night when these lightning bugs are flickering in full force is spectacular. I recall as a small boy collecting fireflies in a jar to get enough light to follow a mountain trail home. They can give off enough light to read by, too.

• *The shrill, ear-shattering noise from a colony of peepers.* Every year, these frogs are out in multitudes announcing their presence. Swamps and ponds are full of them and we delight in hearing their varied sounds. But it always amazes me (even though there's a sound scientific explanation) how these tiny creatures manage to survive the long cold winters of the North Country.

The canoe for me is like a space craft that beams me into another dimension, not toward the stars but into a world of almost unreal beauty and total contentment. I am aware of my film's limitations the moment I snap the camera's shutter. There may be a group of songbirds gathering around me, or the fragrance of balsam and spruce wafting on a morning breeze — elusive qualities that escape even the most glorious photograph. You just have to be there, paddle in hand, to capture the essence of the experience.

**Grand Falls on the
Dead River, Maine**

Paddlers are able to clearly
view this powerful wonder...
and then portage around it.

Lake Champlain, Vermont and New York

The lake is named for Samuel de Champlain who first paddled into the basin in 1609. The Abenaki name for the lake is Bitawbagok or "Lake Between."

Plattsburgh, New York

The city, viewed from a float plane, sits on the shore
of Lake Champlain, at the mouth of the Saranac River.

The canoe for me is like a spacecraft
that beams me into another dimension…
into a world of almost unreal beauty
and total contentment.

Daisies

Flagstaff Lake, Maine

The Appalachian Trail traverses
the nearby Bigelow Preserve
and parallels the Northern
Forest Canoe Trail's waterway
trek across the lake.

Sally Mountain and Big Wood Pond, Maine

Lifting fog reveals Big Wood Pond and creates a halo around Sally Mountain
in this rugged and remote section of western Maine.

Attean Pond, Maine

Attean Pond, which would be called a lake
anywhere else, has clusters of tiny, spruce-tufted
islands and multitudes of rocky outcrops.

Missisquoi River, Vermont

A passing storm enhances and deepens
the summer green of the Missisquoi National
Wildlife Refuge at Mac's Bend.

Jack-in-the-Pulpit

Bluets, also known as Quaker Ladies

Immature Red-Tail Hawk

Great Blue Heron

Raccoon tracks

The track-maker

There may be a group of songbirds…
or the fragrance of balsam and
spruce…elusive qualities that escape
even the most glorious photograph.

Black-eyed Susans

Dead River, Maine

Paddlers navigate the Dead River rapids. The bow paddler here was six months' pregnant, and her son is now a full-grown whitewater canoeist himself.

Morning dew on a grassy bank along the waterway

Luna moth on a balsam
branch after hatching
from its cocoon

Blue damselfly at
the edge of a pond

Moosehead Lake, Maine

Moosehead is the largest lake in Maine. Here, Mount Kineo looms on its eastern shore.

Lake Umbagog National Wildlife Refuge

Habitat and special places are protected in this refuge that manages
more than 20,000 acres on the New Hampshire-Maine border.

Curious frog looks through a spider web.

The swirling vapor forms
twisting columns of mist
wafting upwards
from the water's surface.

Allagash Wilderness Waterway, Maine

A campsite overlooking Round Pond
is warmed by the summer evening sun.

Adirondack Portage. New York

Portage trails, where boats and gear must be carried
from one waterway to the next, are key links on the
Northern Forest Canoe Trail.

Connecticut River, New Hampshire

A high bank on the river near Brunswick, Vermont surprises and delights paddlers traveling this section, offering the sensation of paddling in a sculpted western canyon.

Along the Connecticut River, New Hampshire

Children can be some of the best observers out on the Trail, noticing friends, reptilian and mammalian, all while waiting for lunch.

Top: Sundew; Bottom: Mooselookmeguntic Lake, Maine

Mooselookmeguntic Lake

This vast body of water is surrounded by a cluster of smaller lakes, including Rangeley, Richardson, and Aziscohos. The area has long been a destination for fishermen.

You just have to be there, paddle in hand, to capture the essence of the experience.

GLORY DAYS

Connecticut River, New Hampshire
Autumn sees the Northern Forest in transition.
The glorious color is a gift that one seeks to
store up for the paler winter months.

Previous pages: Adirondack Forest, New York

GLORY DAYS

In the Northeast, autumn is a spectacular season. Bright colors entice "leaf peepers" to the region from throughout the world. Canoeing in the fall can be just as impressive. Anyone with a camera simply can't miss.

But despite the glorious colors and generally comfortable weather, there are usually signs of approaching winter. The days are shorter. And often, a cold snap will leave snowfall on mountain crests and a skim of ice on ponds and backwaters. Photographers think of this as "frosting on the cake".

On one occasion, we landed our canoe at a campsite early because we sensed that the temperature was dropping rapidly. After stoking our campfire for the night, we were about to turn in when I heard what sounded like glass dishes being broken out on the pond. In the gathering darkness, I was able to spot a small branch being towed by a busy beaver working the night shift, preparing his winter food supply. As he swam, the beaver and his cargo were shattering a skim of ice that had already formed on the pond.

Beavers are industrious most of the time, but especially when winter is approaching. A beaver's house is an igloo-shaped mound of sticks and mud with a high and dry interior for raising their family and surviving long cold freezes. Its pond is created for security — a buffer

Lake Champlain, Vermont, seen from New York

Thunderheads can be beautiful, but also serve to alert paddlers that it's time to stick close to shore. A late summer storm can move in quickly, whipping up heavy waves on previously calm waters.

Connecticut River, Vermont shore

When the rains do come in, a tent camp at the river's edge can provide a quick and cozy retreat from the elements.

protecting the only way in through an underwater entrance tunnel. Though they work mainly at night, it is not unusual to see a beaver during the daylight hours.

Beavers' dam-building skills are legendary, but those talents are not always popular with landowners whose streams the pesky and persistent animals have dammed up, flooding fields and drowning trees.

Of interest here, however, is the historical role that beavers inadvertently played in the creation of the Northern Forest Canoe Trail. First, on parts of the trail, seeping water from beaver ponds into various small streams

helped to create the larger bodies of water needed for transportation via the rivers, lakes and bigger ponds. Then, when beaver fur became a popular European and later American commodity, trappers used those routes to deliver their pelts to market.

Although the indiscriminate trapping almost wiped out the beaver population, the plucky little beaver survived. And I consider it a symbolic representation for all the Northern Forest Canoe Trail embodies.

Between Blue Mountain Lake and Eagle Lake, New York

A rustic Adironack bridge is found near the western terminus of the Northern Forest Canoe Trail.

Cathedral Pines Campground on Flagstaff Lake, Eustis, Maine

St. John River, Fort Kent, Maine

At the Northern Forest Canoe Trail's eastern terminus, a homemade traditional bateau plies this broad river that forms the international border between Québec and Maine.

St. Mary's Catholic Church, Newport, Vermont

The church's double spires frame a commanding view
of Lake Memphremagog, most of which lies in Canada.
The Trail's route spans the international border on the lake.

Vermont Sugar Maple

In autumn, bright colors entice
"leaf peepers" to the Northeast
from throughout the world.

Raindrops on delicate spider webs
against a fall foliage background

Dead River, Maine
Flyfishiing at Big Eddy

Following pages: Headwater freshet near Jay Peak, Vermont
Tributaries such as this feed the Missisquoi and other rivers
on the Northern Forest Canoe Trail.

Oseetah Lake, New York

Ruffed Grouse, or Partridge

Osprey

Pileated Woodpecker

Northern Forest Canoe Trail marker

Bull moose

Aster

Canoeing in the fall can
be impressive. Anyone with
a camera simply can't miss.

Top: Northern Maine

Logging trucks are common in Maine's rural landscape today,
but paddlers often see remnants of the time when logs
were sluiced down waterways instead of transported on roads.

Right: Nulhegan River, Vermont

As roads have moved into the north country, the ancient
highways — rivers, streams, and lakes — sometimes
have to incorporate new challenges.

Raquette River, New York

While portaging often looks easy, most paddlers can't
wait to get back on the water. However, the beauty
and power of seeing such features as Buttermilk Falls,
above, are usually worth the extra work.

Barred owl

Northern Forest Canoe Trail feeder stream, Vermont

Float planes out of Greenville, Maine on Moosehead Lake

In remote northern Maine, small planes transport everything from groceries to sightseers.

Saranac Lake village, looking toward the lakefront and the Adirondack high peaks

The Northern Forest Canoe Trail passes right through the village of Saranac Lake, offering paddlers a chance to get supplies, gear, or a warm meal.

Between Lower Saranac Lake and Oseetah Lake, New York

A set of locks eases the way for boaters passing between Lower Saranac Lake and Oseetah Lake

**Upper Ammonoosuc River
Stark, New Hampshire**

A covered bridge spans the
river as the Northern Forest
Canoe Trail route passes
through a scenic village.

Lake Umbagog Nationl Wildlife Refuge, New Hampshire

Despite the glorious colors
and generally comfortable
weather, there are usually
signs of approaching winter.

Migrating snow geese

Maple seedlings

Hardwood forest

These beech and maple trees labor under
the weight of an early snowstorm.

Upper Connecticut River,
New Hampshire

AFTERWORD

Nulhegan River near Island Pond, Vermont

Glimpses of the grand and
intimate nature of the Trail
invite you to experience
its series of destinations.

NORTHERN FOREST CANOE TRAIL

The mission of the Northern Forest Canoe Trail is to celebrate the rich human heritage and diverse natural environment of the Northern Forest by establishing and stewarding a water trail tracing historic Native American travel routes across New York, Vermont, Québec, New Hampshire, and Maine.

The idea for the Trail was born in the 1990s when Native Trails, Inc. researched the traditional east-west water routes used by Native Americans and early settlers in the Northern Forest region. Incorporated in 2000, the Northern Forest Canoe Trail (NFCT) was formed as a way to translate this route research into a recreational, community, and regional resource.

NFCT has distinguished itself as an active, grassroots organization, committed to making the 740-mile Trail accessible for recreation, while being expressive of regional culture and heritage, and economically meaningful to the local communities through which it passes. The Trail is a celebration of both people and place.

In that spirit, we deliver our mission and strategic goals through three program areas:

Waterway Stewardship —
In collaboration with local partners, we initiate and support a range of on-the-ground projects that promote healthy, accessible waterways and riparian areas, and that foster greater connections between residents and their watersheds.

Rural Economic Development —
The Trail passes through more than 40 communities ranging in size from tiny hamlets to mid-sized, bustling towns. Working in tandem with these local partners, NFCT promotes sustainable and nature-based tourism initiatives, whose benefits accrue locally for small businesses and services.

Recreation, Arts, and Heritage —
The waterways of the trail brim with stories about the rich history of the human and natural communities of the Northern Forest region. NFCT supports community-based efforts to share and honor these stories through events, arts projects, and educational programs, and to connect young people to their waterways.

NFCT publishes a 13-map series and a chronicle of the Trail, *Paddling Through Time.* Our book provides a concise review of the historical context that links humans, boats, and water routes in the Northern Forest. Our maps combine detailed route information with interesting area history and stories, enabling paddlers to connect to both the recreational experience and the Trail's heritage. The completion of the map series signified the completion of the 740-mile Trail, a milestone we celebrated with simultaneous events in each of the waterway's four states on June 3, 2006.

The NFCT is not simply a linear water trail; it is a unique linkage of countless and varied experiences. As NFCT founder Ron Canter put it, "The Northern Forest Canoe Trail is a heritage trail — as close as we can come to a time machine. Paddlers jump from the present through many pasts as they slide from wild to rural to urban and back along a thousand-year old water highway."

The images within these pages capture glimpses of the grand and intimate nature of the Trail, and invite you to experience its series of destinations. As you travel the Northeast Passage in this book, we hope you will envision your own experiences on this enticing route.

Kate Williams
Executive Director

Northern Forest Canoe Trail signs

Bull moose

Loon

Beaver

THE NORTHERN FOREST CANOE TRAIL 13-MAP SERIES

1 NORTHERN FOREST CANOE TRAIL — Adirondack North Country (West) NEW YORK — Fulton Chain of Lakes to Long Lake

2 NORTHERN FOREST CANOE TRAIL — Adirondack North Country (Central) NEW YORK — Long Lake to Saranac River

3 NORTHERN FOREST CANOE TRAIL — Adirondack North Country (East) NEW YORK — Saranac River to Lake Champlain

4 NORTHERN FOREST CANOE TRAIL — Islands and Farms Region VERMONT — Lake Champlain and Missisquoi River

5 NORTHERN FOREST CANOE TRAIL — Upper Missisquoi Valley VERMONT/QUÉBEC — Missisquoi River to Lake Memphremagog

6 NORTHERN FOREST CANOE TRAIL — Northeast Kingdom QUEBEC/VERMONT — Lake Memphremagog to Connecticut River

7 NORTHERN FOREST CANOE TRAIL — Great North Woods NEW HAMPSHIRE — Connecticut River to Umbagog Lake

8 NORTHERN FOREST CANOE TRAIL — Rangeley Lakes Region MAINE — Umbagog Lake to Rangeley Lake

9 NORTHERN FOREST CANOE TRAIL — Flagstaff Lake Region MAINE — Rangeley Lake to Spencer Stream

10 NORTHERN FOREST CANOE TRAIL — Greater Jackman Region MAINE — Spencer Stream to Moosehead Lake

11 NORTHERN FOREST CANOE TRAIL — Moosehead/Penobscot Region MAINE — Moosehead Lake to Umbazooksus Stream

12 NORTHERN FOREST CANOE TRAIL — Allagash Region – South MAINE — Umbazooksus Stream to Umsaskis Lake

13 NORTHERN FOREST CANOE TRAIL — Allagash Region – North MAINE — Umsaskis Lake to St. John River

These sectional maps each cover a 40 to 75-mile segment of the trail. They provide interested paddlers with route and interpretive information to help them dip into this storied water trail for an afternoon, a week, or lifetime.

ACKNOWLEDGEMENTS

It is no exaggeration to say that this book has come about almost solely because of the talent and dogged perseverance of Clyde Smith, who is well-known throughout the North Country as a landscape photographer and nature lover. *Northeast Passage* is Clyde's twenty-first book, and getting it into print has been a true labor of love for him. He was inspired to propose the book when the 740-mile waterway, the Northern Forest Canoe Trail, was created. Clyde views the Trail as a perfect way to combine his lifelong love of nature and photography with a similar affection for canoeing. He persuaded Kate Williams, the NFCT executive director, that a photo book about the Trail was not only a good idea but a workable one. And their partnership, along with important financial support from Clyde's good friend, Alice Dodge Wallace and the Avenir Foundation, has been critical in bringing this project to fruition.

But many other folks have played important roles in the development of the Trail and the creation of this book, and they deserve our gratitude and thanks:

Ron Canter, Mike Krepner and Randy Mardres, who hatched the idea that ultimately led to the creation of the Trail and who did much of the early legwork to research its history and map it;

Kay Henry and Rob Center, who built the Trail's organization;

Senators Patrick Leahy, Vermont, and Judd Gregg, New Hampshire, who secured key start-up funding, administered by the National Park Service;

Jennifer Lamphere and Sandy Tarburton, who provided critical logistical support and eagle-eye editing help;

Elizabeth Smith, known to us all as "Lizzie," Clyde's canoeing and life partner, who shepherded us through the entire book-planning process with copious notes and reminders;

Mason Singer, of The Laughing Bear Associates, who designed the book with his usual ultra-professionalism.

And Clyde wants to offer special thanks to his many fellow paddlers who let him position them on rivers and lakes so he could make just the right shot; and to all the cooperative wildlife who allowed their presence to be captured on film.

Thistle Hill Publications is pleased and proud to have been associated with the production of this book.

Jack Crowl
Publisher

NFCT is a non-profit, membership organization.

For information:

Northern Forest Canoe Trail

PO Box 565

Waitsfield, VT 05673

802-496-2285

www.NorthernForestCanoeTrail.org